What's Real, What's Ideal: Overcoming a Negative Body Image

What's Real, What's Ideal: Overcoming a Negative Body Image

Brangien Davis

The Rosen Publishing Group/New York

The Teen Health Library of Eating Disorder Prevention

Published in 1999 by The Rosen Publishing Group, Inc.
29 East 21st Street, New York, NY 10010

Library of Congress Cataloging-in-Publication Data

Davis, Brangien.
What's real, what's ideal : overcoming a negative body image / Brangien Davis.—1st ed.
     p.   cm. — (The teen health library of eating disorder prevention)
"A Hazelden/Rosen book."
Includes index.
Summary: Examines the causes and consequences of negative feelings about one's body and discusses ways to develop a more positive and accepting self-awareness.
ISBN 0-8239-2771-7
1. Body image in adolescence—Juvenile literature. 2. Eating disorders in adolescence—Juvenile literature. 3. Self-perception—Juvenile literature. [1. Body image. 2. Eating disorders. 3. Self-perception.]
  I. Title. II. Series.
RA777.D375 1998
616.85'26—dc21
                                                         98-29941
                                                              CIP
                                                              AC

Manufactured in the United States of America

Contents

Introduction

Sonya and Carly are shopping at the mall. In their favorite store, they pile up armloads of clothes to try on in the dressing rooms. After they put the clothes on, they start yelling over the doors to each other.

"Oh, Carly, nothing fits right. I'm so fat! I have to lose weight."

"You're so much skinnier than me," Carly replies. "My thighs look huge in this skirt!"

"No way. I am such a pig. I'm never eating again."

"Me neither. No wonder Joey hasn't asked me out—I'm totally disgusting."

What do you see when you look in the mirror? The reflection of a happy, healthy young person? Or someone you automatically cut down as too fat, too short, or too ugly? Have you ever thought your whole life would be better if you were thinner and more attractive? These feelings, like those expressed by Carly and Sonya, are examples of negative body image.

How you feel about your body can have a negative effect on how you feel about your entire being.

In today's society, body image is more than just the mental picture you have of what your body looks like. For many, body image is also a reflection of how they feel about themselves and their lives. When people feel bad about their lives, it often translates into feeling bad about their bodies. When they feel out of control in their lives, they try to regain control by controlling their bodies. Their feelings about their body become the way they measure their self-worth.

Your body image is influenced by many different things. It is influenced by family, friends, and a culture that is obsessed with weight, body shape, dieting, and food. All people have negative thoughts and feelings about their body at some point in their life. But when it becomes more than a passing concern, when people base their happiness and self-worth on what they eat, how often they exercise, and how much they weigh, they are suffering from a negative body image. This outlook causes people to believe that all their experiences in life are affected by their appearance and body weight.

Even worse, when this preoccupation with food and weight turns into an obsession, it can result in a full-blown eating disorder. According to Anorexia Nervosa and Related Eating Disorders, Inc. (ANRED), more than 8 million people in the United States are suffering from an eating disorder.

The problems surrounding body image can be especially difficult for teens. Adolescence is a time when you may feel confused about the changes happening to your body. These changes are a natural part of growing up, but they can make you feel out of control and unhappy with your appearance. As a result, you may turn to unhealthy eating habits, which can lead to a serious eating disorder. This can seriously damage your physical and emotional health.

In this book, you'll learn how to recognize a negative body image, what the causes and consequences are, and how to overcome a negative body image. If you work on learning to love and respect your body right now, you'll have the time, energy, and willpower to focus on the most important part of your being—who you are inside.

1

When Angel started high school, it seemed as if everything in her life began to change. She saw less and less of her friends because they were always going out with boys. Angel usually stayed home on Saturday nights thinking that her life would be so much better if she were as thin as the popular girls in school. She was sure she would have as many dates as her friends if she lost weight.

So Angel began a rigid diet and exercise program. She lost a lot of weight in the first few months and people started noticing, complimenting her on her discipline and commitment.

The more she

lost, the more obsessed she became with food. Soon Angel was down to eating only 500 calories a day, cutting all fat from her diet. If she couldn't exercise, she felt like a failure. Angel thought her life would improve if she lost weight, but she felt more out of control than ever before.

People with a negative body image believe that if they don't look right, other things such as their personality, intelligence, social skills, or capabilities also aren't right. They think that if they fix their bodies, all their other problems will disappear. This can result in unhealthy weight management practices and an unhealthy relationship with food. People excessively diet and exercise out of fear of gaining weight.

Nobody is born with a negative body image. It is something that you learn, something that develops over time. As you grow older, your experiences are shaped by the different messages you get from society. And those messages often connect personal success and happiness with being thin and beautiful. If people feel they don't measure up to those ideals of success, then they tend to disregard any other real accomplishments. Having a negative body image can seriously distort the way you look at yourself and your life.

Having a negative body image can be very dangerous if it's not addressed. The good news is, since negative body image is something you learn, it also can be unlearned.

The Ideal

People throughout the world have very specific ideas of what makes someone beautiful. This idea is often referred to as the ideal since it represents what is thought of as perfect. But in many cases, the ideal is impossible and unhealthy for most people to achieve. In the United States, this ideal is constantly promoted through messages and images from the media (advertising, fashion magazines, television, movies).When people don't see themselves in these images, they believe there is something wrong with them. If they constantly judge themselves against this ideal, they will always feel that they're not good enough.

The beauty ideal is always changing. In the 1950s and 1960s, Marilyn Monroe was America's most celebrated sex symbol. But by today's standards, she would be considered overweight and out of shape. Today, the ideal is an impossibly thin, waiflike model who looks nothing like the majority of Americans. But since we are bombarded by these images, people think it's the norm, or standard, for everybody. Ultimately, no matter what the current trend is, the beauty ideal has nothing to do with reality. In reality, people come in a variety of shapes

When fashion designers and advertisers use only thin models in their shows and advertisements, it sends a message to women that thin is the beauty ideal.

and sizes, which are determined mainly by their genetic makeup.

Nonetheless, advertisers in the beauty and fashion industries make it seem that if we don't strive for the beauty ideal, we won't be successful or happy in life. Advertising relies on and targets this feeling of inadequacy to sell products that will supposedly improve our appearance. Advertisers want us to believe the beauty ideal is a goal we can achieve so that we will spend money on products such as fat-free foods, diet drinks, weight-loss pills, skin products, makeup, exercise videos and equipment, and fashion magazines.

Who Has a Negative Body Image?

Anyone can suffer from a negative body image, but it tends to affect females more than males. This is because in our society girls feel more pressure to look good and reach a beauty ideal. At a young age, females are taught to believe that physical appearance is more important than anything else. They believe their physical appearance defines their identity.

In fact, one study conducted by the American Association of University Women found that middle-school girls reported that their looks were the most important factor in feeling good about themselves. A study by Eating Disorders Awareness and Prevention, Inc. (EDAP), showed that young girls are more afraid of becoming fat than they are of cancer, nuclear war, or losing their parents.

Generally, boys are not as vulnerable as girls to negative

With the rising popularity of male models and professional athletes, males, too, are prone to developing a negative body image.

body image. This is because boys are taught by society and their families to define themselves more by abilities than appearance. Boys are encouraged more than girls to express themselves and be aggressive to achieve what they want. But boys, too, can be affected by negative body image. When they don't measure up to an ideal body that is very lean and muscular, they—like girls—may hurt their bodies by overeating or not eating at all.

Experts agree there is a clear connection between negative body image and eating disorders. And since females are more vulnerable to negative body image, they are also more likely than males to suffer from an eating disorder. Ninety to 95 percent of those who suffer from eating disorders are women. But the number of males who have eating disorders is increasing. No one is immune to these problems.

Darius came from a family of athletes. His dad was the football coach at a nearby university and his two brothers were the most popular jocks at school. Darius, on the other hand, loved theater. He belonged to the drama club and had dreams of becoming a playwright. Darius always felt that he had somehow disappointed his father. His brothers teased him a lot about his lack of coordination and the fact that he had never had a girlfriend.

Darius was hurt by his family's comments, but he was too embarrassed to talk to anyone about it. So he kept to himself, staying in his room most of the time reading and writing. Darius began to comfort himself with food. He would carry up boxes of doughnuts and bags of potato chips to keep him company. Soon Darius was bingeing every night. After every binge, he felt disgusted with himself because he had no control over his eating, and he was gaining weight.

Do I Have a Negative Body Image?

It's important to recognize the signs of a negative body image. Once you recognize the problem, you can work on accepting your body. The sooner you address the problem, the more likely you are to overcome it.

- Are you afraid of getting fat?
- Do you think about food a lot?
- Do you constantly compare your body with those of others?
- Do you say negative things about your body to other people?
- Do you say mean things about your body to yourself (in your head)?
- Do you get mad at yourself or your body after looking at magazines or watching television?

When you don't feel good about yourself, it can lead you to isolate yourself from your friends. You may not be inclined to participate in social activities, particularly those involving food.

❏ Do you avoid social activities because you think others will find you unattractive?

❏ Do you avoid eating around other people?

❏ Do you wish you could change the way you look?

If you answered yes to most of these questions, negative body image is affecting your life and you should consider getting help. Without help, you may be putting yourself at risk for an eating disorder.

The Causes of a Negative Body Image

Can you remember a time when you didn't worry about what your body looked like? For most of us, early childhood was a time in our lives when we played and ran and experienced life—without concern for what we looked like or what we ate. We thought of food as fuel for our bodies. We ate when we were hungry and stopped when we were full. So what happened? When did we start to think constantly about how we look to other people? And when did we start paying so much attention to food, mirrors, scales, clothes, and magazines?

The answers are not simple and for every person they can be different. Sometimes negative body image can be triggered by one definite event, other times it can arise gradually, for a combination of reasons. In this chapter, some of the many possible causes of a negative body image are discussed.

Puberty

"When I turned thirteen, my skin started breaking out and I gained weight, especially on my thighs and stomach. I hated the way I looked. I would spend hours looking in the mirror. I stopped going out with my friends. It got so bad that I sometimes thought about killing myself."

Puberty is a time when young bodies become adult bodies. As you enter puberty, your body goes through a number of changes. You may feel out of control because your body seems to be doing things you've never felt before—some of which are uncomfortable or embarrassing.

Females naturally gain weight during puberty (ages nine to sixteen). This is the body's way of preparing for menstruation and childbirth. Hips start to widen, breasts begin to develop, and body fat increases. It's all part of the process of becoming a healthy woman. But these physical changes can sometimes trigger negative body image because of all the images of very thin women and advertisements for diets and weight-loss products that surround us. For males, too, puberty can be a troubling time if their bodies don't achieve a very lean and muscular ideal. As a result, young women and men who dislike their bodies may begin to diet.

Adolescence is one of the most stressful times of life, when you deal with countless physical changes as well as social pressures. It's a time when fitting into a group can feel very important. Teens always know what is "in" and "out," so it becomes important to adhere to the societal ideal. You may even think if you reach the ideal, you'll be accepted and liked by everyone.

However, just when it seems important to fit in, it is also the most dangerous time to diet. Adolescent bodies are growing and developing into healthy adult bodies—and they can't do it without proper nutrition.

The Beauty Industry

"I was so obsessed with how fat I was that I constantly compared myself to every girl on television, in magazines, even in cartoons! All I could think about was how much bigger I was compared to all those other women. It was so depressing that I stopped going to school. Instead, I stayed in my room and slept all day."

You see them everywhere—perfect, beautiful women and men. Anywhere you look—magazines, television, movies, even video games—you can't get away from seeing females and males who either look like or actually are fashion models, staring you down and making you feel less than perfect.

But the truth is, these "perfect" models look this way for many reasons. First of all, they are usually wearing heavy makeup (even to achieve the "natural" look)—so much that you probably wouldn't even recognize models if you saw them on the street without their makeup. Special camera angles and lighting add to the illusion of perfection.

Most pictures of women in fashion magazines are airbrushed. This means that after the photo is taken, professionals use special tools to correct any imperfections that show up in the photo and might make the model look less than ideal (or more like a normal human being!). Another popular trick is altering a photo with computers to achieve a perfect image. Another important fact to remember about women and men we see in the media is that many of them have had plastic surgery. In addition, some may actually be starving themselves in order to stay thin.

It's also important to recognize that society is filled with images of perfection because the beauty ideal sells. Advertisers promote the beauty ideal as if it

were the real thing because they believe you will spend and spend to try to reach the ideal.

Think about all the things you can buy that promise to make you thinner or have better skin, softer hair, whiter teeth, or bigger muscles. The beauty industry wants you to buy perfume, low-fat foods, exercise equipment, cosmetics, and clothes. Fashion magazines push the beauty ideal the hardest because they want to sell magazines as well as the products advertised inside.

The beauty industry is harmful because it tricks people into

Advertisers send strong messages to convince people they need to buy things that will improve their life, such as new beauty products.

spending money on products that won't really help them meet the beauty ideal (since it is a physical impossibility). And it's almost impossible to escape the beauty industry's messages. They are everywhere. Accepting them and believing in them can severely damage your feelings about your body and yourself. A study done in 1995, for example, found that after just three minutes of looking at a fashion magazine, 70 percent of women interviewed felt depressed and guilty.

Families and Food

"When I was young, my dad would make comments about how much I ate. He would tease me and say, 'Lorena's on a seafood diet. She sees food and eats it!' I know he was only joking, but it hurt. It made me really self-conscious around food."

As with many other important issues you encounter, your family has a lot of influence on how you feel about food and your body. As you grow older, food takes on different meanings. Parents tell us what is good to eat and when and how much we should eat. Even though we learn that candy and sweets are bad for us, we receive such foods as rewards for good behavior. These mixed messages about food can create some complex eating problems.

Family behaviors around eating habits can have an impact on body image, especially for females. If you

Your family strongly influences your attitudes toward food and your body. If meals were relaxing and didn't focus on how much someone did or didn't eat, you are likely to have a healthy attitude about eating and your body.

see your mother always worrying about her weight, going on and off diets, it sends a powerful message and may make everybody in the family believe that worrying about weight is normal and expected.

Families also can cause negative body image if parents have unreasonably high expectations for their children. These expectations can make us feel inadequate, depressed, or guilty when they don't match our interests. You may take your frustrations out on your body through dieting or excessive exercise as a way to assert control over your life.

Peer Pressure

During adolescence, your friends can have a tremendous influence on what you think and do. Peers become very important as you struggle to find your own identity. As you become more independent from your parents, your friends are the ones you go to for approval and acceptance.

But your peers can put a lot of pressure on you to conform to society's standards. And much of the time this pressure can be mean and cruel. It may even seem as if hating your own body is the hip thing to do. Girls often engage in fat talk, complaining about their bodies, always finding fault with them. As Mary Pipher wrote in *Reviving Ophelia*, "Girls punish other girls for failing to achieve the same impossible goals that they are failing to achieve." If all your friends talk about how fat and ugly they think they are, you may begin to feel the same.

Unfortunately, this kind of talk feeds off itself, becoming an unhealthy cycle that is difficult to break. Even worse, your friends can encourage you to engage in unhealthy behaviors. Many girls learn about eating disorders from their friends and compete to be the thinnest or the smallest.

Low Self-Esteem

Another factor that may lead to negative body

image is low self-esteem. Self-esteem is the way you feel about yourself and your abilities. People with high self-esteem have confidence in their capabilities, and they like themselves the way they are. Those with low self-esteem have serious doubts about what they can achieve and often feel too scared to try new things because they fear they will not succeed.

Self-esteem is very difficult to measure, and it's also hard to figure out exactly where it comes from, but one thing is sure: self-esteem is closely related to body image. Research has shown that females suffer from low self-esteem because they think they are not desirable or beautiful. This means they believe their self-worth is dependent upon how others view their bodies and their looks.

Regardless of what anyone looks like, it is important to remember that how you feel about yourself influences how other people react to you. If you are comfortable with who you are and how you look, others will be too.

Surrounding yourself with good friends who are positive people can help build your confidence. Knowing that people like you and accept you for who you are can help you get through times when you are feeling down.

Research shows that before age ten girls are more emotionally and physically confident than boys. But as they hit the teen years something starts to change. Girls start to lose their self-confidence at the same time their bodies begin to change. This connection results in an intense focus on their bodies. When they don't receive acceptance from others about how they look, they suffer from low self-esteem and begin to question their self-worth.

Sexual Abuse

Some research has shown that negative body image can be caused by sexual abuse. When sexual abuse occurs, especially at a young age, the victim may experience a great deal of discomfort with his or her body. The body serves as a reminder of the horrible experience, and he or she may feel responsible for the abuse. As a consequence, victims of sexual abuse may think of their bodies as objects to be despised and punished.

Another way sexual abuse may play a part in causing negative body image is that girls who are sexually abused at a young age may be afraid of entering puberty and becoming women. Victims may worry that looking more like a woman will bring more abuse. So these girls may starve themselves in hopes of stopping the development of their bodies and menstrual periods, which are a natural part of womanhood. Victims may be believe that if they stay thin, their abuser will leave them alone.

Sexual abuse is a serious crime. If you feel you have been sexually abused, it is essential that you find a trusted adult you can talk to privately about your experiences. Instead of punishing yourself with negative body image, if you are a victim of sexual abuse try to take steps to get the help you need and deserve.

No Easy Answers

Negative body image is a very complex issue. Ultimately there is no single cause or single cure. No one intentionally develops a negative body image.

It's often an unconscious process in response to larger issues in a person's life. Overcoming a negative body image involves addressing those larger issues. Without looking at the underlying problems, teens may be in great danger of hurting themselves.

How a Negative Body Image Affects the Body and Mind

Negative body image is dangerous because it can lead to many other mental and physical health risks. It can be the first stop on the way to depression, self-mutilation, unhealthy eating habits, and serious eating disorders. Eating disorders are a growing problem among teenagers. And 80 percent of eating disorders started with a diet.

Dieting

When people feel unhappy with their bodies, they usually feel a diet is the answer to their problems. And this idea is reinforced everywhere by our society.

Americans spend billions of dollars every year on the diet industry. Dieting is such a common practice in the United States that many girls believe it to be a rite of passage in life. But dieting has negative mental and physical consequences. Dieting means restricting the amount of food you eat. Your physical health suffers because your body doesn't get all the nutrients it needs. When losing weight is the ultimate goal, people begin to define themselves by a number on a scale. They may forget that there are many other qualities that define a person. Qualities such as intelligence, honesty, and a sense of humor are overshadowed by how much a person weighs and what a person looks like.

The Dangers of Dieting

The body needs a certain amount of calories every day. The food we eat is converted into fuel for the body to carry on its normal functions. When we do not provide the body with this necessary fuel, it tries to conserve fuel by slowing down its rate of metabolism. Metabolism is the rate at which the body burns calories. When this rate is lowered, it means the body burns fewer calories and stores fat more efficiently.

When you eat less, the body responds by holding on to any food it gets. When a person goes off the diet, the body will regain all, if not more, of the weight lost during the diet. This is because the metabolism rate does not return to normal after a diet.

In addition to being ineffective, dieting also can physically damage the body—especially the body of a growing teenager. The teen years are a time of great mental and physical growth. During this time, the body is changing from a child's body into an adult's body. The body needs all the right nutrients to make this transformation successfully. When the body doesn't receive them, it will not be able to develop properly. Important bodily functions, such as a young woman's menstruation, may be delayed. A lack of nutrients, such as calcium, also can lead to osteoporosis later in life. This disease causes a decrease in bone mass. The bones weaken and break easily. During the teen years, a lack of calcium can increase the risk of stress fractures.

Another danger of dieting is the attitude it can create. When a diet is unsuccessful, a person's self-esteem suffers. He or she may feel like a failure when weight

The endless cycle of going on and off diets is known as yo-yo dieting. Yo-yo dieting can slow your metabolism and make you tired and moody.

is not lost permanently. He or she can begin an unhealthy cycle of yo-yo dieting. Yo-yo dieting is when a person begins and quits a diet several times. A person may focus all his or her attention on losing weight. He or she may begin to lose touch with reality and become desperate in the quest to lose weight. Taking diet pills or other weight-loss products is only the beginning of an unhealthy pattern of behavior. This pattern may eventually lead to the development of an eating disorder.

What Is an Eating Disorder?

Eating disorders include anorexia nervosa, bulimia nervosa, and binge-eating disorder (compulsive eating). Compulsive exercise is also a growing problem and classified by experts as a related eating disorder problem. A person can have one or more of these disorders, and anyone can suffer from them—men and women of all ages and from all walks of life.

Anorexia Nervosa

Anorexia nervosa is usually shortened to anorexia. Although the word "anorexia" means "loss of appetite," the opposite is true. Those with anorexia are hungry all the time. Their weight is at least 15 percent below normal for their height and age. They are starving themselves, sometimes to death. But those with anorexia fear putting on weight and

No matter how thin a person with anorexia becomes, he or she is never satisfied with their appearance. Sadly, these people are putting themselves at risk for numerous and often irreversible health problems.

often see themselves as heavier than they really are. Anorexia causes many physical problems. Because the body has so little fat, it can't maintain a normal body temperature. As a result, fine hairs, called lanugo, grow all over the body to try and keep it warm. People with anorexia are frequently cold, even in summer. Girls with anorexia suffer from amenorrhea, which means that menstrual periods stop. Near-starvation and the resulting lack of calcium may cause osteoporosis later in life. Starvation also weakens the heart, which can develop a slow or irregular beat. Loss of fluids can cause dehydration. Dehydration can lead to an electrolyte imbalance in the body, causing death.

Anorexia also causes emotional problems. Because people who suffer from anorexia tend to isolate themselves from family and friends, they may suffer from depression. Lack of food can harm the person's ability to think straight and concentrate. It can also cause a person to feel irritable, unhappy, and pessimistic most of the time.

Bulimia Nervosa

Bulimia nervosa, or bulimia, is characterized by binge and purge cycles. Bingeing is eating a large amount of food in a short amount of time. Purging is when a person tries to rid the body of the food by vomiting, using laxatives to bring on a bowel movement, abusing diuretics to increase urination, and abusing drugs that induce vomiting. Some people exercise excessively to rid the body of the calories.

Bulimia causes many health problems as well. These include dry skin and hair, brittle nails, or bleeding

Eating disorders, such as bulimia and anorexia, weaken the body. This, in turn, affects physical and mental performance. Teen athletes are particularly vulnerable to eating disorders.

gums. The teeth develop cavities or ragged edges from stomach acids brought up by frequent vomiting. Vomiting also puts tremendous strain on the stomach and esophagus. When the lining of the esophagus breaks down, an ulcer develops. Purging gets rid of food before nutrients are absorbed. Without these nutrients, the body can suffer from malnutrition.

In addition, repeated use of laxatives can cause painful constipation (an inability to have bowel movements). Abusing diuretics can cause dehydration. Using ipecac syrup to induce vomiting is extremely dangerous and can cause congestive heart failure and death.

Bulimia can cause the same emotional problems that people with anorexia develop. Because people who suffer from bulimia keep their binge/purge cycles a secret, they can feel isolated and alone and suffer from depression. Fifty percent of those who suffer from bulimia have struggled, or continue to struggle, with anorexia.

Compulsive Eating (Binge Eating Disorder)

Compulsive eaters (sometimes called compulsive overeaters) are people who eat in response to psychological stress. In doing so, they eat when they're not hungry. Like those with bulimia, compulsive eaters go on food binges. Some compulsive eaters graze, eating many times during the day or night. People who compulsively overeat may wish to lose weight, but they do not purge food from their bodies.

Compulsive eating is psychologically damaging because people use food as a way to deal with uncomfortable feelings. Because they may not feel safe expressing sadness, anger, or other emotions, they eat as a way to find comfort. Also, most people with this disorder are overweight and may be at risk for other health problems, such as heart disease and diabetes. Being overweight alone does not always cause health problems, but it can be a problem when combined with an inactive lifestyle.

It's important to remember that the symptoms of these eating disorders can be interchangeable. Keep this in mind if you are concerned that you or someone you love has an eating disorder. Here are some general warning signs to watch for.

Eating Disorder Warning Signs

Some common signs of eating disorders are:

- ❑ Constantly thinking about the size and shape of your body
- ❑ Constantly thinking about how much you weigh and repeatedly weighing yourself
- ❑ Constantly thinking about food, cooking, and eating
- ❑ Eating only certain foods in specific and limited amounts
- ❑ Wanting to eat alone and feeling uncomfortable eating with other people
- ❑ Not feeling good about yourself unless you are thin but never being satisfied with how thin you are
- ❑ Feeling that you should exercise more, no matter how much you already exercise
- ❑ Feeling competitive about dieting and wanting to be the thinnest or the smallest
- ❑ Keeping a list of what foods are okay to eat

- Taking diet pills or abusing laxatives and/or diuretics
- Continuing to diet, even after you are thin
- Purposely losing lots of weight very quickly
- Forcing yourself to throw up
- No longer having your monthly period

You'll notice that some of the above warning signs of an eating disorder are similar to the signs of negative body image. This is because negative body image is closely linked and can lead to eating disorders. Negative body image is on a continuum, or a range, of severity. People who suffer from negative body image are more likely to have an eating disorder as well. They usually go hand in hand. Keep in mind that you don't have to have every symptom on this list to suffer from negative body image or to have an eating disorder. If some of these signs seem familiar to you, please consider speaking to a trusted adult and getting help.

Self-Mutilation

I have so much negative emotion inside of me. I don't know how to get rid of it all. I cut myself because it's easier to deal with the physical pain. Watching the blood is like watching all my hateful feelings wash away. I go into the bathroom and look at myself in the mirror. All I can think about is how ugly I am and how much I hate myself. Then I start cutting my arms or my legs, and I don't stop until I feel calm again.

It has many names: self-injury, self-injurious behavior, self-abuse, self-cutting, and repetitive self-harm syndrome. It is most often called self-mutilation. Regardless of what name you use, it is the intentional destruction or alteration of one's own body tissue without conscious suicidal intent.

Self-mutilation includes many acts such as cutting, skin carving, burning, scratching, bone breaking, picking scabbed wounds, and trichotillomania, or plucking eyelashes, eyebrows, and hair from the scalp.

Most often self-mutilators are female and are likely to suffer from an eating disorder as well. There are many reasons why people cut, burn, or engage in other self-injurious acts. It can be a way to convert unbearable emotions into tolerable physical pain. Some people say they self-mutilate because they are emotionally numb and it helps them feel something. Others say it helps them express anger or release tension.

Self-mutilation, eating disorders, and a negative body image are very difficult issues. Those who suffer may not think it's right or normal to express

People suffering from a negative body image are prone to self-harming behaviors such as an eating disorder and even self-mutilation. When someone engages in either, it's important to seek professional help.

feelings, such as anger or rejection. But feelings aren't right or wrong, they just are. Learning to cope with and express them is a big part of understanding who you are.

The road to recovery from an eating disorder or self-mutilation can begin with simply reaching out to a trusted friend or family member. With that person's encouragement and the help of a mental health professional, you can reclaim your life.

Recovery

Eating disorders and self-mutilation are serious matters. They can permanently damage the body, and a person can also die from an eating disorder or self-mutilation. Even with professional help, it takes a long time to recover, but many people do and go on to live successful, healthy lives.

If you think you may be suffering from one or more of these eating disorders, it's important that you reach out for help. Talk to someone you trust and seek professional help. Consult the list of organizations in the Where to Go for Help section at the back of this book. You can contact one or more of them for more information and resources. Only then can you begin to recover from the disorder and take back control of your life.

Finding Peace with Your Body

4

At first I didn't think talk-ing about my problems would help. But it really does. It wasn't easy and I can't say that I'm 100 percent better, but my attitude has definitely changed. For the first time in a long while, I can say that I'm happy with who I am.

Even after you learn about the dangers of having a nega-tive body image, it isn't always easy to prevent it or over-come it. It's hard to ignore or even fight against the negative messages you receive every day. But you are not powerless against this problem. There are many ways to stop the habits and behaviors that contribute to a negative body image and many ways to help you find peace with your body. It may be the hardest thing you ever do, but it's one of the most important things you'll ever do for yourself.

Changing your body image is a process that you will have to work on for many years, if not the rest of your life. The most important thing to remember is that recovery comes through changing your attitude, not your body. Feeling good about yourself is the key to making healthy decisions about how to care for and celebrate your body.

Change can begin by simply educating yourself—reading books and contacting organizations that deal with the dangers of the beauty ideal, negative body image, and eating disorders. But if your problems are more serious, you will need to seek more help.

Getting Help

Because having a negative body image is an indication of larger problems in your life, treatment must involve attacking the causes behind it. This can involve psychological counseling, which will help you deal with emotions in a healthy way. It's very important to learn how to handle stress, anger, and frustration without taking it out on your body. Both individual therapy and

If you don't know how to find the help you need, reading up on your problems can help. Books, newspaper articles, and even your local phone book are all good places to find out where to get help.

group therapy are positive ways to accomplish this. Look in the Where to Go for Help section of this book for organizations that can direct you to more resources, or talk to a trusted adult or friend.

You may also benefit from a support group. There are many support groups around the country that offer a confidential and comfortable atmosphere to discuss your problems with people who have similar feelings and experiences. If there isn't one in your area, you can start your own. See the Where to Go for Help section for ideas on where to look in your area.

Nutritional Counseling

Having a negative body image often results in

unhealthy eating patterns. Speaking with a registered dietitian at your school or family clinic about food and nutrition will help you understand why your body needs food, vitamins, and minerals to function properly. You'll learn why your body needs fat in order to stay healthy also. You'll learn that eating a variety of different foods is healthy, and that eating in response to hunger rather than emotional needs will help you reach your goals.

A registered dietitian can help you relearn normal eating patterns. Ellyn Satter, author of *Child of Mine: Feeding with Love and Good Sense*, writes, "Normal eating is flexible. It varies in response to your hunger, your schedule, your proximity to food, and your feelings. Normal eating takes up some of your time and attention, but keeps its place as only one important area of your life."

Why Weight Doesn't Matter

Having a negative body image often means a person spends most of his or her time focusing on weight. Part of finding peace with your body means changing your focus. Knowing a little bit about genetics can help you do that.

Everyone has his or her own individual set point of weight. This set point is the weight your body naturally falls to when you eat well and exercise regularly. It varies from person to person, much like hair color or

Try to engage in physical activity on a regular basis. Any activity—in-line skating, a pickup game of basketball, walking, or playing Frisbee—will help you stay healthy.

eye color. This set point is determined mostly by your genetic makeup. This means that your body shape and size are established by the genes you inherited from your parents. You have only so much control over how much you weigh and what your body looks like.

In addition, many experts are starting to believe that overall health is more important than your weight. Your health depends more on how much you exercise and what kinds of foods you eat than on how much you weigh. In other words, it's not fat that matters, it's fitness and health.

It's important to exercise because it keeps your body healthy, not because it burns calories. Otherwise you risk becoming obsessed with your exercise routine. Moderation is the key. The Centers for Disease Control and Prevention and the American Council on Sports Medicine recommend about half an hour of moderate exercise three or four days a week. But that doesn't mean you need to go to extremes. Exercise should be fun, something you enjoy. The types of activities you do can vary, from riding a bike to gardening or even cleaning up your room!

This information can help you begin to accept your body shape and to appreciate yourself and other people for their unique qualities. Weight is not only something you have little control over, but you can be perfectly healthy if you eat right and get regular exercise— no matter how much you weigh. As you stop focusing on your weight and body shape, you can begin to spend time on more creative things in your life.

Keep a Journal

As you begin to incorporate changes in your life, you may find that keeping a journal is a good way to see how you've progressed. Your journal is a place that is all yours. You can write as much or as little as you'd like. It's a place to record your thoughts and feelings. It's a good idea, however, to pay attention to negative talk. The point of keeping a journal is to identify the things that trigger negative feelings. If you are having negative feelings, try to counter them with positive statements. Try to remember that your goal is to change your focus and work on developing a positive body image.

Generating Awareness About Body Issues

5

I finally realized how bad I felt after reading all those fashion magazines. I started thinking, Why does everybody look the same? I looked at the people in my life and realized how different everybody was. Why wasn't my reality represented? I found the address of the magazine in the letters section and wrote down my thoughts. To my surprise, the letter was printed! All my friends thought it was pretty cool. We decided to start a letter-writing campaign. It felt good to fight back and to know I could make a difference.

Many people feel that fighting back against society's unrealistic ideals helps people change their own ideals. Speaking out and fighting back can provide a release for all those negative thoughts. Taking action can increase your self-confidence and give you a sense of purpose. There are people and organizations fighting against negative media messages. Join them in their efforts and you will begin to see results.

Be a Critic!

One way to feel better about your body image is to become a critic. Think about the fact that advertising executives are trying to get you to buy their products. They want you to believe that if you buy their product, you will look just like the models in the advertisements. But you know that these ads are not representations of reality.

Every time you see an ad that starts to make you feel bad about your body, stop and think: What does this advertiser want me to think? (That the model is beautiful and I should look more like her.) What is this advertiser trying to get me to do? (Spend my money on the products in the ad.) Why would the advertiser want me to believe the beauty ideal is real? (So they can make millions of dollars!)

Bust Stereotypes!

Once you start to look at the beauty industry with a

If you see an advertisement that features idealized, unrealistic images of people and it bothers you, let that company know. Write a letter to them or visit their corporate Web site and send your comments via e-mail.

critical eye, you can begin to reject the beauty ideal as the big lie that it is. After all, how many real people do you know who look anything like the models we see in magazines and on television?

You are a valuable consumer to advertisers. They care about what you think because they want you to buy their products. If you see an advertisement, a movie, a music video, or anything else that you don't like or that encourages the stereotype that thin is good and fat is bad, use your voice and speak out. In addition, if you see messages that promote positive and diverse images of men and women, write letters to those companies to tell them you support their efforts.

Promote a Positive Message

Help your friends recognize that healthy bodies come in many shapes and sizes and express appreciation for diversity. Instead of vowing to each other that you'll never eat again, why not start your own positive body image/high self-esteem club? Get together and talk about all the great things you do that have nothing to do with how you look.

You can work on changing family attitudes, too. Don't participate in name-calling based on appearances. Compliment family members for their accomplishments (as well as their looks). Share information about the dangers of dieting and eating disorders. And encourage high self-esteem in your whole family by showing appreciation and love for all family members.

Creative Exercises That Really Help

It isn't easy to develop a positive body image. It takes time. But here are some exercises that can help you on your journey.

- Before you say negative things about your body, ask yourself if you would ever say these words to a friend or loved one. If you wouldn't say such mean things to others, why is it acceptable to say them to yourself? If you see a part of your body you don't like, think about why you feel it is unacceptable and who benefits from your thinking this way.

❏ Make a list of all the wonderful things your body makes possible every day—whether it's singing, walking, dancing, playing sports, or giving someone a hug.

❏ Change the critical voice inside your head that talks down to you. When you start to think negatively about yourself, stop and look at what you are thinking, ask yourself what triggered the feelings, and then challenge what you are saying to yourself. Take the time to repeat your good qualities to yourself every day.

❏ Write a letter to yourself talking about all your excellent abilities that have nothing to do with how you look. Don't be shy—read it out loud in front of the mirror! Or make a list of your best friend's top ten qualities that don't have anything to do with appearance, and ask him or her to do the same for you. Then mail them to each other.

Talking with friends about how they feel about themselves can be an enlightening experience. You might be surprised to find that they too have days when they feel less confident. The key is learning to put your bad feelings in perspective and know that they will soon pass.

❏ Make a list of friends and family members you admire. Write down what it is besides their appearance that makes them so special. Aren't these people more inspiring role models than those you see in the fashion magazines?

❏ Set goals for yourself that have nothing to do with how you look. Get involved in different clubs or activities and explore your various interests. Write down all of your achievements—including both tiny and huge ones—and congratulate yourself for each one.

❑ Express yourself and all your creative qualities! Stop comparing yourself to others. Keep a journal, paint a picture, write stories, make a craft, play an instrument—whatever it takes to remind yourself that there is much, much more to you than how you look.

These exercises will benefit anyone, no matter where they fall on the negative body image continuum. It's important to remember, though, that if you are suffering from an eating disorder, it's absolutely necessary to seek professional help. Help is out there if you want it and are ready to accept it. Talk to someone you trust, and know that you can and will get better.

Glossary

adolescence Preteen and teen years of a person's life when a person is changing from a child into an adult.

dehydration The process of losing water or bodily fluids.

depression Feelings of sadness and hopelessness that last a long period of time.

eating disorder An unhealthy and extreme concern with weight, body size, food, and eating habits.

electrolyte imbalance A life-threatening condition in which a person doesn't have enough of the minerals the body needs to maintain healthy fluid balance.

esophagus A muscular tube that connects the back of the mouth to the stomach.

genetic Influenced by genes, which we inherit from our parents and which determine physical traits.

menstruation Female monthly bleeding sometimes called a period.

nutrients Vitamins, minerals, and other food ingredients that your body needs to stay healthy.

obsession A persistent and disturbing preoccupation with an unhealthy or unreasonable idea or feeling.

psychological Having to do with the mind.

puberty The time when your body becomes sexually mature.

role model A person you can look up to and admire for who they are and the things they have done.

self-esteem Confidence, self-respect, and satisfaction with oneself.

stereotype An oversimplified opinion based on general or limited information.

Where to Go for Help

The American Anorexia/Bulimia Association (AABA)
165 West 46th Street, Suite 1108
New York, NY 10036
(212) 575-6200
Web site: http://members.aol.com/AMANBU

Anorexia Nervosa and Related Eating Disorders, Inc. (ANRED)
P.O. Box 5102
Eugene, OR 97405
(541) 344-1144
Web site: http://www.anred.com

Eating Disorders Awareness and Prevention, Inc. (EDAP)
603 Stewart Street, Suite 803
Seattle, WA 98101
(206) 382-3587
Web site: http://members.aol.com/edapinc

National Association of Anorexia Nervosa and Associated Disorders (ANAD)
P.O. Box 7
Highland Park, IL 60035
(847) 831-3438
Web site: http://members.aol.com/anad20/index.html

National Eating Disorders Organization (NEDO)
6655 South Yale Avenue
Tulsa, OK 74136
(918) 481-4044
Web site: http://www.laureate.com

National Association to Advance Fat Acceptance (NAAFA)
P.O. Box 188620
Sacramento, CA 95818
(800) 442-1214
Web site: http://www.naafa.org

S.A.F.E. (Self-Abuse Finally Ends)
40 Timberline Drive
Lemont, IL 60439
(800) 669-2426
Information line: (800) DONTCUT (366-8288)

In Canada

Anorexia Nervosa and Associated Disorders (ANAD)
109-2040 West 12th Avenue
Vancouver, British Columbia V6J 2G2
(604) 739-2070

The National Eating Disorder Information Centre
200 Elizabeth Street
College Wing, 1st Floor, Room 211
Toronto, Ontario M5G 2C4
(416) 340-4156

S.A.F.E.
306-241 Simcoe Street
London, Ontario N6B 3L4
(519) 434-9473

Web sites

http://www.about-face.org
(A group that fights negative and distorted images of women)

http://www.gurze.com
(An extensive eating disorders resource catalog with related links)

http://www.melpomene.org
(An organization dedicated to women's health and physical activity)

http://www.something-fishy.com/ed.htm
(Web site with a huge amount of information on eating disorders and body image)

http://www.the-body-shop.com
(The Web site for The Body Shop, which works to improve the self-image of people everywhere)

http://www.palace.net/ ~ llama/psych/injury.html
(Web site that offers resources and help for those struggling with self-mutilation)

For Further Reading

Cooke, Kaz. *Real Gorgeous: The Truth About Body and Beauty*. New York: W. W. Norton and Company, 1996.

Fraser, Laura. *Losing It: America's Obsession with Weight and the Industry That Feeds on It*. New York: Dutton, 1997.

Freedman, Rita. *Bodylove: Learning to Like Our Looks and Ourselves*. New York: HarperCollins, 1990.

Hall, Lisa F. *Perk!: The Story of a Teenager with Bulimia*. Carlsbad, CA: Gürze Books, 1997.

Hornbacher, Marya. *Wasted: A Memoir of Anorexia and Bulimia*. New York: HarperCollins, 1998.

McCoy, Kathy and Charles Wibblesman. *The New Teenage Body Book*. New York: Perigee, 1992.

Pipher, Mary. *Reviving Ophelia: Saving the Selves of Adolescent Girls*. New York: Ballantine Books, 1995.

Rodin, Dr. Judith. *Body Traps: Breaking the Binds that Keep You from Feeling Good About Your Body*. New York: Quill, 1993.

Simmons, Cassandra Walker. *Becoming Myself: True Stories About Learning from Life*. Minneapolis, MN: Free Spirit, 1994.

Index

About the Author

Brangien Davis received a master's degree in public policy and women's studies from George Washington University in Washington, D.C. She makes her home on the West Coast.

Design and Layout: Christine Innamorato

Consulting Editor: Michele I. Drohan

Photo Credits

Photo on p. 7 © Laurie Bayer/International Stock; p. 13 © UPI/Corbis-Bettman; p. 14 © Jim Whitmer/FPG International; p. 17 © Stephanie Rausser/FPG International; p.18 © John Terence Turner/FPG International; pp. 22, 26 by Seth Dinnerman; pp. 24, 30 © Ron Chapple/FPG International; p. 27 © Navaswan/FPG International; p. 32 © Arthur Tilley/FPG International; p. 34 © Dick Luria/FPG International; p. 36 © Jill Sabella/FPG International; p. 41 by Brian Silak; p. 42 by John Bentham; p. 44 ©Michael Krasowitz/FPG International; pp. 46, 52 by Ira Fox; p. 48 © Chuck Mason/International Stock; p. 50 © Michael Paras/International Stock; p. 55 © Jay Thomas/International Stock.